S0-AYS-916

Sinatra
Frank and Friendly

A UNIQUE PHOTOGRAPHIC MEMOIR OF A LEGEND BY
TERRY O'NEILL

MORE THAN 100 PHOTOGRAPHS SPANNING 20 YEARS, BACKSTAGE, ON LOCATION, AND IN PRIVATE. EDITED BY
ROBIN MORGAN

PUBLISHERS EVANS MITCHELL BOOKS

The Old Forge, 16 Church Street, Rickmansworth, Herts WD3 1DH, United Kingdom info@senateconsulting.co.uk

WWW.EMBOOKS.CO.UK

© Evans Mitchell Books. Printed 2007 **TEXT & PHOTOGRAPHS** © Terry O'Neill **EDITOR** Robin Morgan **DESIGN** Darren Westlake at **TU ink** www.tuink.co.uk **PRINTER** Advance Agro Print Center, Thailand **ISBN** 1 901268 32 2 **&** 9 781901 268324.
All rights reserved. No part of this book may be reproduced in any form or by any means, or stored in a retrieval system, or transmitted electronically or mechanically, or photocopied, without prior permission in writing from the Publisher, except by a reviewer who may quote brief passages for review. The right of Terry O'Neill to be identified as the author of this work has been asserted by him in accordance with the Copyright, Design and Patents Act 1988.

MOST OF THE PHOTOGRAPHS IN
SINATRA: FRANK & FRIENDLY
HAVE NEVER BEEN PUBLISHED BEFORE

TOGETHER WITH TERRY O'NEILL'S PERSONAL
MEMORIES OF THE TIMES THEY SPENT
TOGETHER, **SINATRA: FRANK & FRIENDLY**
IS TERRY O'NEILL'S PERSONAL HOMAGE
TO THE MAN AND HIS MUSIC

For five decades **TERRY O'NEILL** has chronicled the frontline of fame. His photographs have hung in national museums and art galleries worldwide; they are treasured by art collectors and have graced the covers of every major magazine in the world from *Time*, *Life*, and *Newsweek* to *Cosmopolitan*, *Premier* and *Rolling Stone*.

Doors beyond the reach of his peers open for Terry O'Neill. He has photographed monarchs, presidents and princes; he has dined in the White House and Buckingham Palace and photographed the foremost people of our time; First Lady Laura Bush chose O'Neill to take her inaugural portrait inside the White House; HM Queen Elizabeth II and Princess Diana of Wales ranked him as one of their favourite portrait photographers.

He has counted stars of stage, screen, politics, sport and rock 'n roll on both sides of the Atlantic, as personal friends. He was photographing The Beatles and The Rolling Stones when they were still barely boys. O'Neill has a gift for identifying star potential – he picked out a 14 year old girl called Jodie Kidd on a beach in Barbados and launched her catwalk career. His photography made him an intimate of icons such as Ava Gardner, Brigitte Bardot, Raquel Welch, Michael Caine, Paul Newman, Michael Douglas, Catherine Zeta Jones, and Faye Dunaway. All invited him "inside", behind the limelight of their celebrity.

Sinatra
Frank and Friendly

is a testimony to that trust, and O'Neill's discerning eye. Images capturing a relationship that spanned three decades, take us behind the scenes of Sinatra's incredible journey. The superstar of music and movies allowed O'Neill's camera to follow his every move, on the road, at home and backstage.

In the age of papparazi, doorstep photography, and big-budget publicity shoots, O'Neill's fascinating archive of his relationship with Sinatra reminds us there was once a golden age, when the stars and their audience where intimate and inseparable.

A break in filming, Frank lights up beneath a portrait of Raquel Welch. Years later Frank smoked a pipe – it was easier on his vocal chords than cigarettes **TON**

Terry comments:

"He adored women. They were all ladies to Frank. He said 'I'm supposed to have a Ph.D on the subject; I admire them. But like all men, I don't understand them.'"

Detail, detail, detail. Frank had a huge work ethic. It was the musician in him, his search for perfection transferred to the movie set ᴛ ᴏ'ɴ

"I HAVE AN OVERACUTE CAPACITY
FOR SADNESS AS WELL AS ELATION.
I'VE BEEN THERE – AND BACK.
I GUESS THE AUDIENCE FEELS IT
ALONG WITH ME. THEY CAN'T HELP
IT. SENTIMENTALITY, AFTER ALL,
IS AN EMOTION COMMON TO
ALL HUMANITY"

"YOU ONLY LIVE ONCE
AND THE WAY I LIVE
ONCE IS ENOUGH"

Terry comments:

*"He was one of those actors
who fitted the part like a glove
— on stage he had huge empathy with the music
and the mood, but put a gun on his hip
and he suddenly transformed
into the good cop
with the hard attitude."*

He loved doing impressions and he was a brilliant mimic – Cagney was a favourite **T O'N**

I caught him deep in thought minutes before the curtain call – he liked to take a moment to collect his thoughts т о'n

Frank relaxes at the piano as his make-up man details the day's schedule for filming *Lady In Cement* in 1968

Terry comments:

"Following Frank around was a photographer's dream. There was this air about him — as if he was immortal and you didn't want to miss an opportunity to capture him on film."

Frank had a constant companion. He called him the Emperor. His real name was Michael Gergenson but he was the proprietor of Romanoff's, the Beverley Hills restaurant Fra

loved. He was a father figure to Frank **T O'N**

The Lady In Cement 1968. Raquel Welch was a nervous young actress. The director Gordon Douglas credited Frank with putting her at ease T O'N

He was impeccable in his manners towards a lady. But he loved to make them laugh and Raquel Welch laughed a lot on the set of *Lady In Cement* T O'N

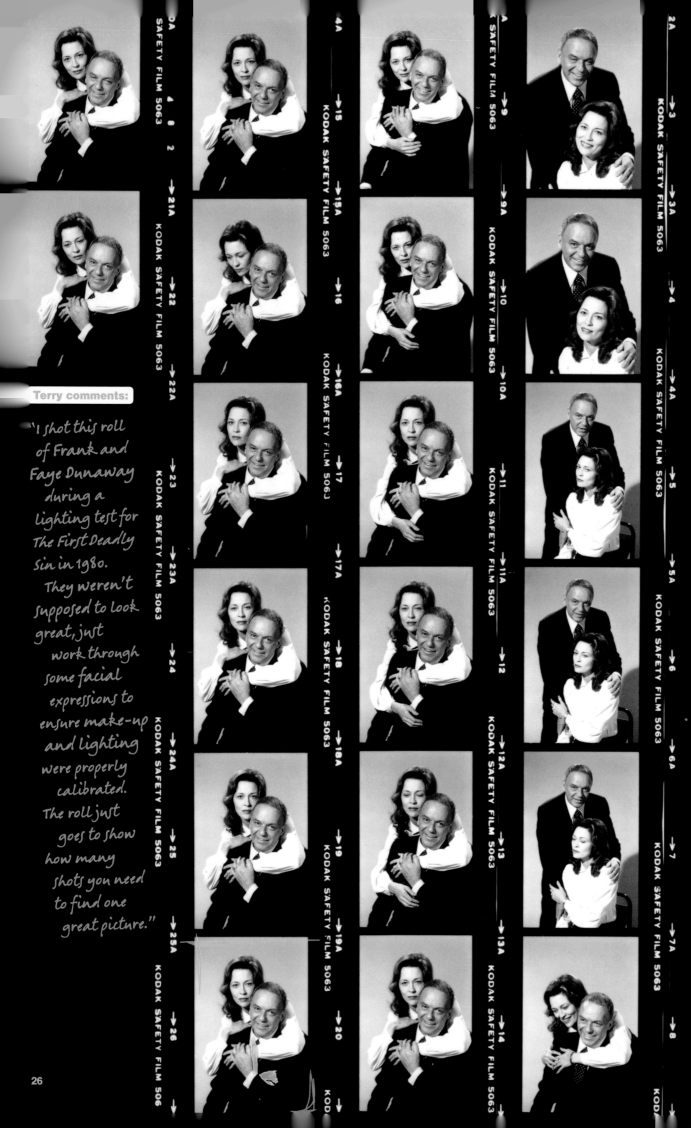

Terry comments:

"I shot this roll of Frank and Faye Dunaway during a lighting test for The First Deadly Sin in 1980. They weren't supposed to look great, just work through some facial expressions to ensure make-up and lighting were properly calibrated. The roll just goes to show how many shots you need to find one great picture."

26

Relaxing between takes, on set with colleagues in Miami 1968 **T O'N**

**"WE'RE ABOUT TO SING
THE NATIONAL ANTHEM
– BUT YOU NEEDN'T RISE"**
FRANK WAS REFERRING
TO MY WAY

Princess Margaret was a huge fan – she knew every song, every lyric. Frank fascinated her T O'N

Terry comments:

*"The First Deadly Sin
with Faye Dunaway in 1980
was Frank's first movie for 10 years
– it was a great role for him,
the tough guy and
the sensitive
grieving husband."*

Diahann Carroll on a US TV show

"I'M NOT OLD ENOUGH TO UNDERSTAND ADULTS BUT I THINK I KNOW ENOUGH TO UNDERSTAND KIDS"

Kids always got Frank's attention – he had time for them T O'N

Terry comments:

"He did a week long gig at the Royal Albert Hall
with Sarah Vaughan and Count Basie.
350,000 people applied for the 15,000 tickets.
Touts were selling tickets
at 10 times their face value
— and this was 1975."

"SAMMY DAVIS JR ONCE SAID
'I WANTED TO BE LIKE HIM SO BAD...'
WHO DIDN'T"
TERRY O'NEILL

Terry comments:

"I never got the three of them together, so I photographed Sammy, Dean and Frank separately and put this montage together just for myself."

Terry comments:

"This was a guy who played golf with Princes and Presidents. I remember someone presenting him with this set of handmade clubs and the delight was written all over his face. Each club was monogrammed, even the balls."

Terry comments:

"He played and practised his swing with them every second he got off camera."

"STAY ALIVE, STAY ACTIVE,
AND GET AS MUCH PRACTICE
AS YOU CAN"

It didn't matter if he was on the golf course or at the pool table – he was always very competitive

Sinatra, stunt double and bodyguards walk along the Miami boardwalk to the set of *The Lady in Cement*

Terry comments:

"Frank on the boardwalk is one of my most memorable Sinatra photographs.
But when I look at the rolls of film I took that day in 1968 there are so many iconic shots that stand alone."

"MARLENE DIETRICH
ONCE CALLED HIM THE
**'MERCEDES-BENZ
OF MEN'"**
TERRY O'NEILL

"Raquel Welch was
in and out of the pool
all morning to get the
scene right,
but Frank stayed on set,
reassuring her,
putting her at
her ease."

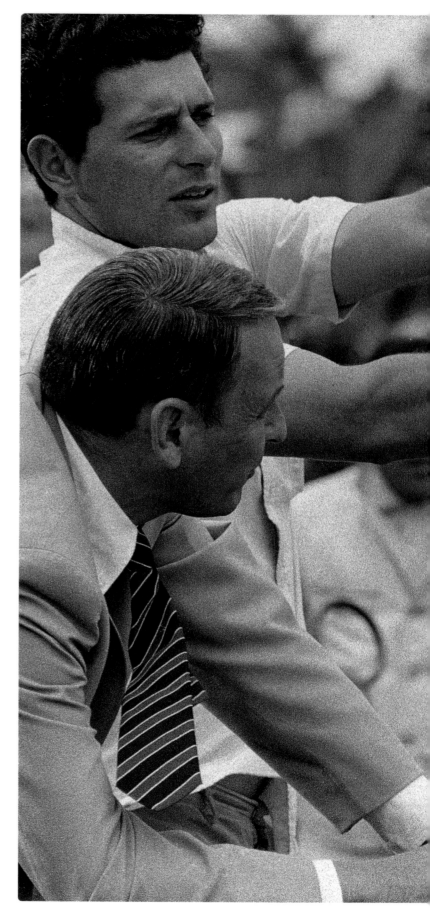

"During the shooting of Lady In Cement, the director Gordon Douglas worked Raquel hard but Frank stood up for her and gave her confidence."

Terry comments:

"He phoned me up at four in the morning
and said he was going to shoot me.
His 'boys' actually scoured London for me all night.
He'd seen a photograph he didn't like
in a newspaper and thought it was one of mine.
I still don't know to this day
if he was serious."

Some scenes called for some heavy duty action – I was amazed Frank put himself on the line instead of using his double

"Dan Blocker – Hoss Cartwright
   from the TV series Bonanza
was a big man, 300lbs and 6ft 3.
       He played a murderous thug
who hires detective Tony Rome
   (Frank) to find a girl."

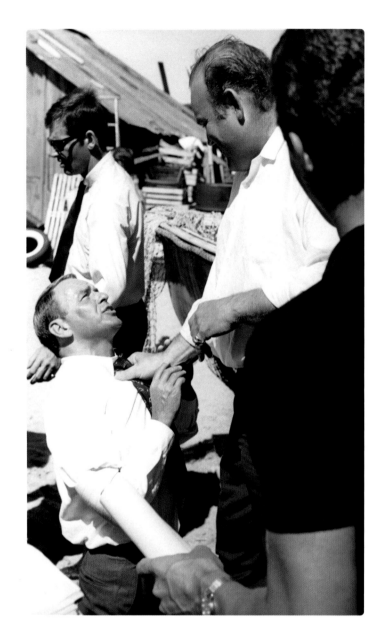

Terry comments: "Dan actually had a small part in a Frank Sinatra movie, Come Blow Your Horn, five years earlier, but Lady in Cement was his big break from TV into movies. Sadly he died quite young, four years later."

"They had a lot of laughs. Blocker looked so intimidating but he was at heart a big guy with a big heart and they had a lot of fun together fooling around and entertaining the cast."

Terry comments:

"On the set of Deadly Sin Frank was supposed to be visiting his dying wife Faye Dunaway but it was hard to stop them laughing between takes."

"Frank's sense of humour was legendary. Dean Martin who feared flying told a story. He'd been invited to accompany Frank on a tour:

"WE'RE UP ABOUT 35,000 FEET AND FRANK HANDS ME A CHEQUE FOR A LOT OF MONEY
'WHY DIDN'T YOU GIVE ME THIS ON THE GROUND?'
'BECAUSE' HE SAID
'YOU WOULDN'T HAVE GOTTEN ON THE PLANE THAT'S WHY'"

There was a wonderful rapport with the comedian Pat Henry who had to dress up in drag for a scene in *Lady In Cement*. Off camera it was a hoot T O'N

Remember this was the 60s – a big burly guy in a bra, blonde wig and cigar? It raised a lot of laughs off set when Pat teetered in on his heels

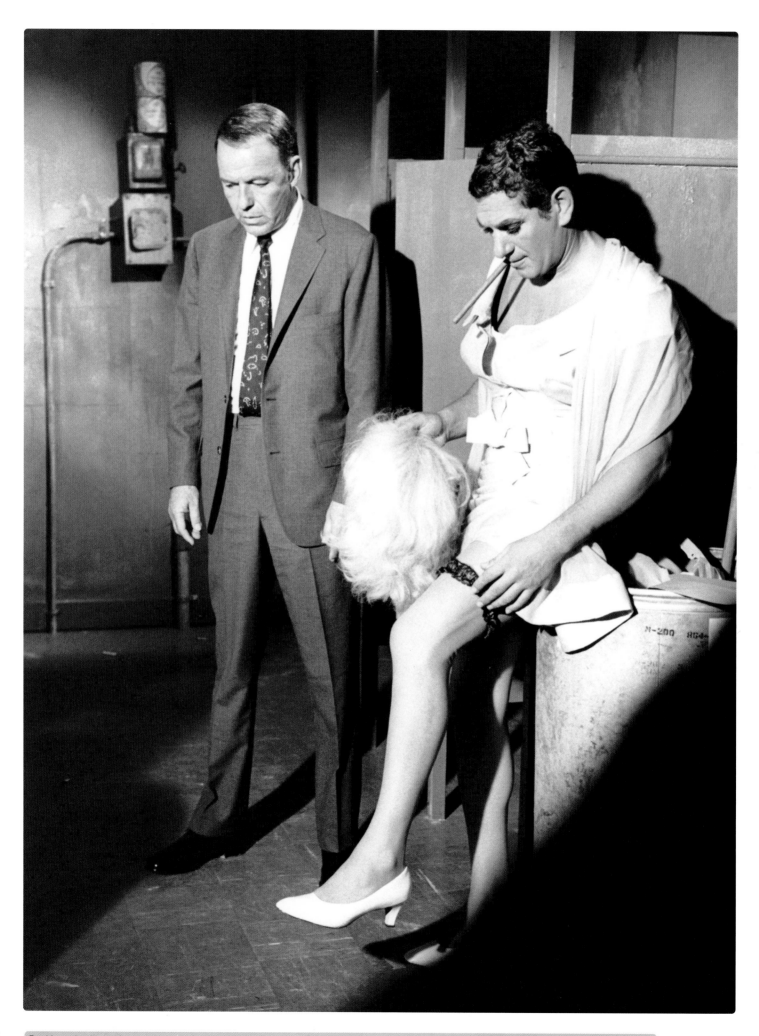

Pat Henry had actually played Andy Capp in a TV series – but the character was transported from England to Boston for US audiences **T O'N**

Frank could flick a switch on set. One minute joking around and the next, straight into character as the tough guy T O'N

Terry comments:

"This has to be one of my most surreal pictures ever — I still crack up everytime I see it. You can imagine this scene prompted a lot of horseplay between two alpha males."

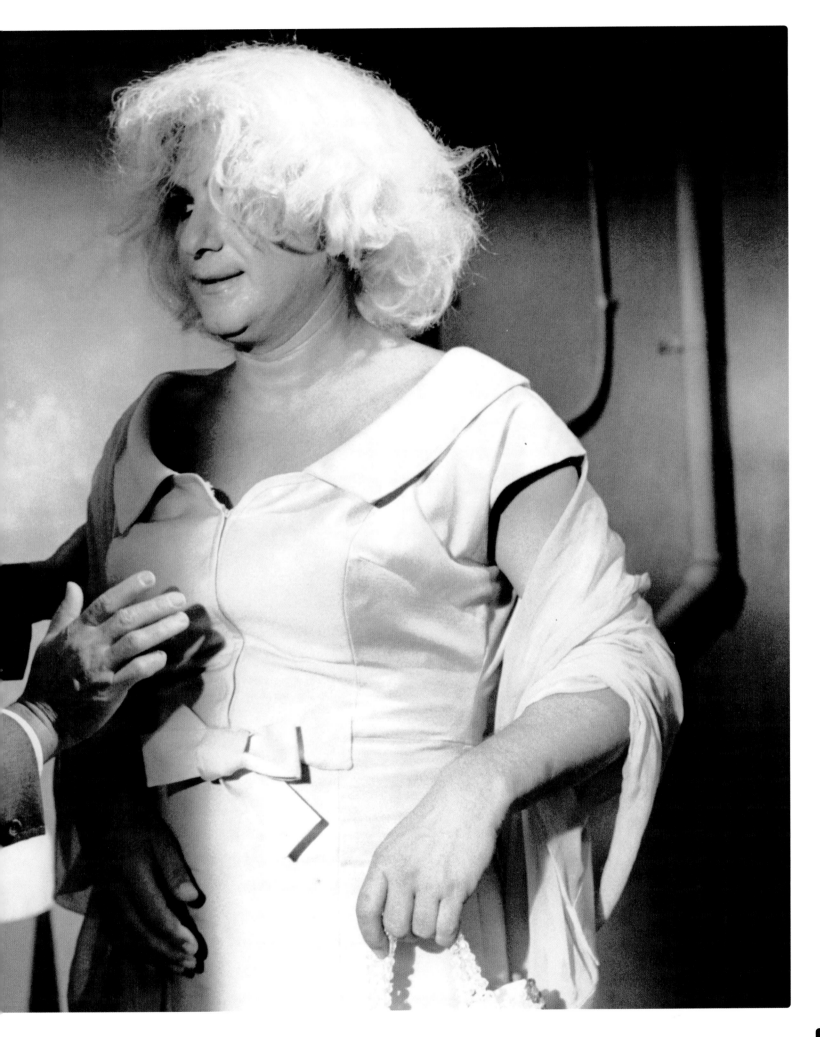

I never saw him lose his temper or act impatiently with musicians. He worshiped music; Jazz was in his soul T O'N

"He was rehearsing the orchestra at the London Palladium in 1989 and I suddenly noticed he was smoking a pipe. In 20 years I'd only ever seen him smoke cigarettes."

"IF I CAN FIND THE TIME
I'D LIKE TO DO A LONG SERIES
OF ONE-NIGHTERS, ALL OVER THE COUNTRY
I'D TAKE AN ORCHESTRA, LIKE BASIE
AND A FEW OTHER PERFORMERS
AND JUST SING FOR AN HOUR OR TWO
CONCERT-STYLE
IT WOULD BE FUN"

He treated every detail as if it was a musical note – everything had to be pitch-perfect T O'N

"He toured the world in 1976. It's incredible to remember he played 140 concerts to over half a million people and he was 60 years of age."

"IF THE SONG IS A LAMENT
AT THE LOSS OF LOVE
I GET AN ACHE IN MY GUT.
I FEEL THE LOSS MYSELF"

He invariably worked with his arranger, Bill Miller, the pianist and band leader – they knew each other's moves and moods inside out

"One of the British sax players who worked with Sinatra said
'We loved rehearsals – he was the guy –
aura, charisma, magic. We'd work through the numbers
with him, he always treated us well.'"

Rehearsals weren't just work, they were adventures, Frank and the musicians exploring the limits of the music and lyric, pushing the boundaries

"I'VE SUNG WITH THE BEST, AND I'VE HAD IT ALL.
I'VE GONE FROM NEIGHBORHOOD SALOONS TO CARNEGIE HALL.
AND THE EXPERIENCE I HAVE TO SAY WAS GRAND.
BUT I COULDN'T HAVE MADE IT WITHOUT THEM –
HERE'S TO THE BAND..."

"I ALWAYS SANG A TOUGH BOOK, YOU KNOW. IT USED TO WRING ME OUT"

Terry comments:

"I was often mesmerised not just by his voice but his body
— the way he moved to the music,
as if every muscle was invisibly tuned to emphasise the song."

"I'd be everywhere taking photographs, on stage, in the wings, in the pit,
always on the move but he never blinked,
he was too intent on getting it right."

"I'VE SEEN THAT FACE BEFORE
THAT FACE IN THE MIRROR
I KNOW THAT FACE
I'VE SEEN THAT FACE BEFORE
I KNEW THAT DOPEY GUY
WHEN HE DIDN'T KNOW
HOW TO TIE HIS TIE
HE STOOD RIGHT THERE
AND HE HAD HAIR GALORE!"
THE MAN IN THE LOOKING GLASS
FRANK SINATRA, 1965

Terry comments:

"It couldn't happen today – a photographer
wouldn't be allowed the access and
the freedom to be around a star
as big as Frank Sinatra.

But he knew my job was as important to me
as his music was to him and he respected that,
allowed me the same environment to work in
that he would demand for himself."

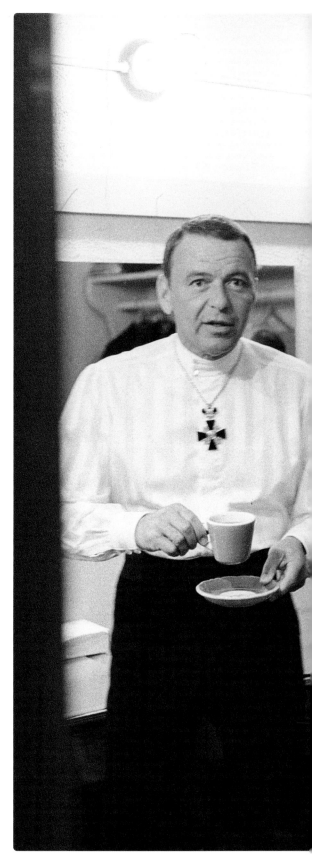

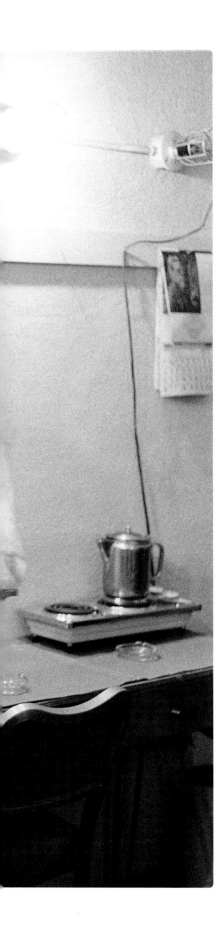

"AS I APPROACH THE PRIME OF MY LIFE
I FIND I HAVE THE TIME OF MY LIFE..."
THIS IS ALL I ASK
FRANK SINATRA, 1965

Terry comments:

" I love this picture – it says everything about the
man – surrounded by people before
a big concert with the camera on him,
he remained cool, wrapped up in his preparations
for the evening's performance."

Terry comments:

"He liked honey and lemon in his tea before a show.
He was singing on average three times a week
for nearly a year at this stage of his career
and the brew helped soothe his vocal chords."

"Backstage everything was laid out,
from his suit and shirts to his aftershave.
But he always prepared himself for a performance.
He had to be immaculate,
how he looked was as important
as how he sang."

Live on Stage

Terry comments:

"These days 'stars' work six weeks
on a movie, three times a year
and say they're exhausted.
He'd spend all day on the set
doing a movie and then go on stage
that night to perform.
And he'd do that day after day.
He made nearly 60 movies,
100 albums and over
2,000 singles."

"Sometimes you didn't bother looking for one great shot of Frank. You needed to see a whole roll together on a contact sheet — as if every frame was a note in the number he was singing."

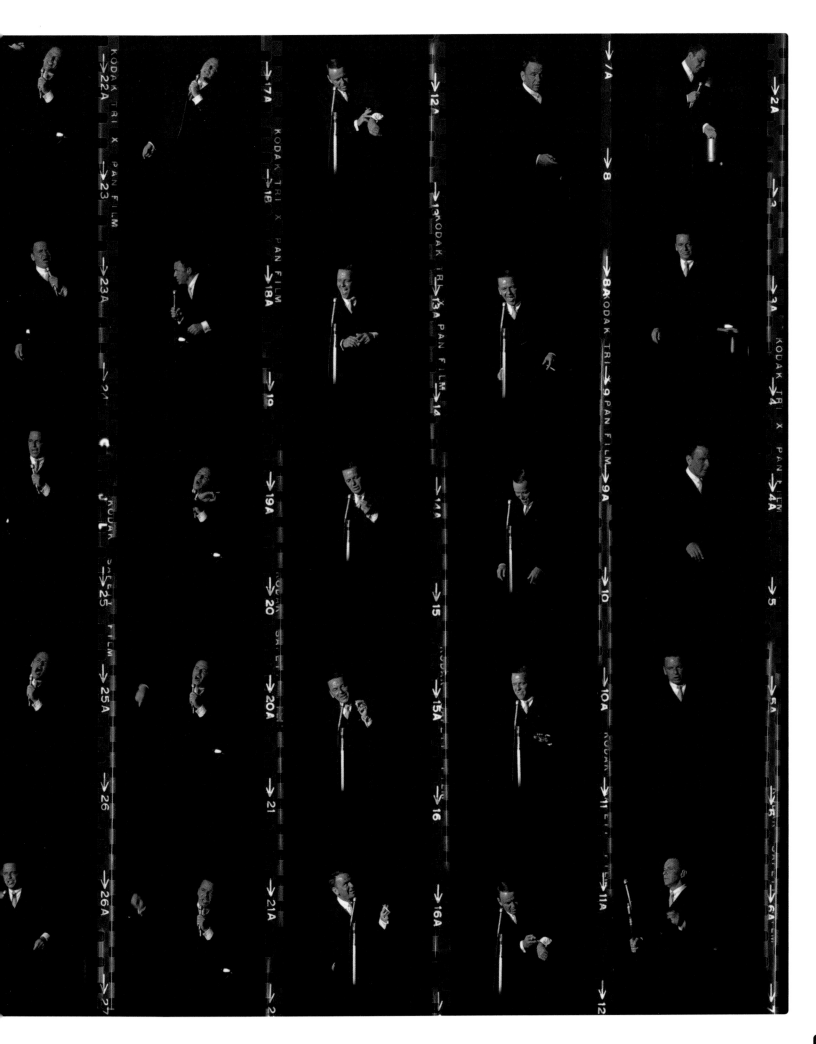

"I THINK I GET AN AUDIENCE INVOLVED PERSONALLY IN A SONG –
BECAUSE I'M INVOLVED. IT'S NOT SOMETHING I DO DELIBERATELY
I CAN'T HELP MYSELF"

Terry comments:

"He judged his audience every night.
He'd stand in the wings during the warm up
and watch them, analyse their mood and then
tailor the act to their needs, knowing what
they'd want the second he stepped
in front of them."

Terry comments:

"I'd watch him move, graceful, commanding, like a big cat on the prowl, ruling his kingdom. Such was his charisma, every step he took seemed to be important somehow."

Terry comments:

"Every time I watched him perform I couldn't get over the fact that this was an extra-ordinary guy who just lived to be on stage and sing for people — nothing else mattered quite so much as being up there for an audience."

Terry comments:

"Some nights he couldn't wait to get out on stage. He felt the clamour and thrived on it. It wasn't nerves it was excitement."

"Every picture in this strip tells a story – I never published any of them because I couldn't choose one over the others. All I remember was shooting film, after film, after film – I didn't want to miss a moment of him on stage."

"Thank you for letting me sing for you" he told his audiences. And he meant it. He lived to please them ᴛ ᴏ'ɴ

"The bands and orchestras loved working with him because he never forgot to applaud them and their part in the show."

"People would run down the aisles,
to hand him flowers, bottles of Scotch,
to kiss his hand, or just touch his shoe.
He never shirked from them.
He hugged them, he kissed them.
He let no-one come between them,
it was intimate, like a love affair
between Frank and his fans."

Terry comments:

"On stage everything seemed so effortless.
It was only once the curtain fell
that you realised
how much energy he'd exhausted
on stage."

Terry's final comment:

"When I look back on our times together I remember Miami in 1968.
He'd arrive on the set at noon, work through till seven at night
then go back to the Fountaineblean Hotel and prepare for a concert.
And he did that day after day, week after week.
Think about his career; the Oscars, the No 1 singles, the hit albums,
scores of movies, thousands of concerts –

nobody will ever come close to Frank."